River *of* Words

Poems selected by
Robert Hass & Pamela Michael

Art selected by
Thacher Hurd

**Annual Poetry & Art Contest
On the Theme of Watersheds**

In affiliation with
The Library of Congress Center for the Book

This book is made possible by a generous grant from the
United States Environmental Protection Agency
Department of Water

Our Funders
Berkeley Civic Arts
Christensen Fund
Compton Foundation
Global Community Foundation
Walter & Elise Haas Fund
New Belgium Brewery
Nightingale Family Fund
Panta Rhea Foundation
Potrero Nuevo Fund
Samantha Sanderson
San Francisco Estuary Project
US EPA
Wood Foundation

NATIONAL
ENDOWMENT
FOR THE ARTS
A great nation
deserves great art.

Our Wonderful Volunteers
Izabela Akerman, Brenda Hillman
Charles Legere, Marilyn Martin
Dave Seter

Our Hard-Working Interns
Joel Brown, Pepper Luboff,
Molly Meyer, Gabrielle Myers

Our Kind, In-Kind Donors
Glen Billy
Keith Whitaker & Marian O'Brien
Susan Brooks, Jeweler
Carie De Ruiter, MIG Communications
Mel & Angie Dagovitz
Thacher Hurd
Michael Mack

ROW Staff
Pamela Michael, Executive Director, Co-founder
Louisa Michaels, Program Manager
Susan Sarratt, Outreach Manager
Max, Office Dog

ROW Board of Directors
Robert Hass, Co-chair, Co-founder
Samantha Sanderson, Co-chair
Chris Anderson   Christina Batt
Rebecca Black   Carie DeRuiter
Ben Grumbles   Susan Kirshenbaum
Kim Knox   Bettina Ring
Jane Rogers   Mary Selkirk
Becky Su   Jessica Trogler
Erin Van Rheenen   David Wood
Stanley Young

And special thanks to Southwest Airlines for flying our winners and their families to the River of Words Award Ceremony at The Library of Congress in Washington, DC. Southwest's commitment to the environment has won them many awards from US EPA and other regulators; they have been in the forefront of such efficiencies as paperless tickets, quick turnarounds, installation of winglets, and, more recently, the installation of fleet-wide advanced avionics.

This book is lovingly dedicated to

JIM AND WILETA BURCH

Creative Earth Stewards Extraordinaire

Jim and Wileta Burch have been supporting and inspiring the non-profit education world for decades. Their love of the natural world and their commitment to protecting it is lifelong; the assistance they have given countless organizations like River of Words has been crucial and, in many cases, transformative.

Though Californians for over a half century, they both hail from the heartland—Jim from Illinois and Wileta from Kansas. Through their creative projects, community service, good counsel and philanthropy they've embraced the West, indeed the planet, and contributed mightily to its people, institutions and culture.

Wileta is a painter of uncommon sensitivity to the natural world. In addition to her painting, she leads educational seminars for youth and adults. Jim was Mayor of Palo Alto, California and served on the City Council for many years. He began a radio career during World War II as part of the Armed Forces Radio Service in occupied Japan and later went on to write for radio and television. After working in advertising for over twenty years, he left the corporate world to begin a second career with Wileta as a volunteer activist, working with such pivotal organizations as Creative Initiative Foundation, World Beyond War and Project Survival.

While working with the Foundation for Global Community, Jim and Wileta produced a vibrant and educational series of video documentaries, which are offered to public television stations free of charge, on a variety of topics relating to the earth and sustainable living: Children and Nature, The Living Land, Water: Sacred and Profaned, A Sense of Place, Art of the Wild.

The lifelong work of this remarkable couple is a tribute to the power of love, shared vision, collaboration, and the gift of community service.

River of Words: The Language of Landscape

Connecting Kids to Their Watersheds and Their Imaginations

> There was a child went forth every day. And the first object he looked upon,
> that object he became. And that object became part of him for the day or a
> certain part of the day. Or for many years or stretching cycles of years. The
> early lilacs became part of this child. And grass and white and red morning
> glories, and white and red clover, and the song of the phoebe-bird.
>
> —Walt Whitman

At one time in the United States, not too many generations ago, virtually everyone grew up knowing what watershed they lived in. Rivers then were our only interstate "highways;" most still ran wild across the landscape and in our imaginations. We celebrated the central role they played in our lives in story and song—"Red River Valley," "Oh Shenandoah," *Life on the Mississippi*. Children spent much of their time outdoors, exploring the world around them—searching knee-deep in creeks for tadpoles, building forts in empty lots, weaving daisy chains, collecting rocks, climbing trees. Their experience of the natural world was visceral, frequent, and fun. This investigative, hands-on approach to learning is what River of Words has spent the last fourteen years re-introducing to the educational process. One look at the art and poetry in these pages—so full of energy and place—affirms the wisdom (and astonishing success) of our mission.

Nature has been the greatest source of inspiration for artists and poets since humans began drawing animals on the walls of caves. Most of what we know of ancient cultures has been gleaned from the artistic expressions they left behind. Yet despite the manifest importance of the arts and the natural world they seek to interpret, the state of both art and environmental education in the United States reflects their marginalized status. Our forests and rivers are tallied as resources; the arts are considered peripheral at best, a self-indulgent frivolity. Decades have passed since botany, geography, or natural history was paid more than rudimentary attention in classrooms, and fewer than half our elementary schools have full-time art teachers.

This devaluing of the very fundamentals that sustain, define, and nurture us—our land and our creativity—has already robbed many of our children of a true sense of belonging to a particular place. Few of them have any real knowledge of where their tap water comes from, where their garbage goes. They know little of who lived on their land before they did and what songs and stories they created, what art the landscape inspired. Few American schoolchildren can name more than a handful of the plants or birds in their own neighborhoods, yet studies have shown the average child can identify over one thousand corporate logos. This sorry scenario is increasingly true in other countries as well, even those that still value the role of art in society.

River of Words released its first "Watershed Explorer" curriculum in 1995. Our place-based approach to teaching art and science in tandem was hailed as innovative and particularly effective in getting students excited about learning. Our novel curriculum combined kite making and flying with the study of wind, atmosphere, birds and aerodynamics. We coupled sketching and botany, natural journaling and poetry making, for instance, allowing children to explore topics creatively, using both left-brain and right-brain skills.

Because both art and science rely on observation and reflection, pattern recognition, experimentation, and critical thinking, we were surprised they weren't taught together more often. While revising and expanding our curriculum, however, poring over old textbooks for ideas, we realized our curriculum wasn't new after all: turn-of-the-century natural history texts were brimming with art, poetry, songs, and even a splash of spirituality. There was a sweetness, a respect and love for nature and beauty in these earlier lessons that seemed worth emulating, especially in a world so lacking in these qualities.

I remember finding my mother's childhood botanical sketchbooks in a trunk when I was eight or nine. They were a beautiful and complete rendering of the northern Illinois flora of her youth. I looked forward to the time in my own schooling when I would create a similar record of South Carolina's plants. That time never came: botany and plant identification somehow fell into a pedagogical crack in the 1950s, destined to become quaint, old-fashioned teaching relics, like the practice of memorizing poems. "Once upon a midnight dreary, while I pondered, weak and weary......" Almost fifty years later, reciting that old chestnut still bestows a warm pleasure. How many of today's children will have an opportunity to experience that same familiar comfort? How many will have the skills, knowledge, and imagination they will need to address the daunting environmental and social problems that twenty-first century living will certainly thrust upon them?

Bob Hass and I started a poetry and art contest for children on the theme of watersheds with the hope that focusing students' attention on their own homegrounds would give them an informed understanding of place that would help them grow into active citizens. We sought to nurture creativity and promote the idea that while not everyone can be an artist, everyone can be artistic. We've tried to add elements of wonder, discovery, interpretation, dexterity, and surprise to learning—natural history treasure hunts in schools; oral history projects at senior centers; visits from local birders, farmers, artists, poets or newspaper editors. Our small and hopeful idea has grown into a program that trains hundreds of teachers each year and touches the lives of tens of thousands of children annually. Hundreds of communities participate in River of Words-inspired art exhibitions, creek clean ups, watershed festivals, poetry readings, award ceremonies and celebrations. Can there be any doubt that education is the key to sustainable living, tolerance, and cross-cultural understanding?

"Beauty will save the world," Fyodor Dostoevsky said. We offer the thoughtful and heartfelt creations in this book from the children of the world as our best hope for the future.

—*Pamela Michael*
River of Words Executive Director & Co-founder

TABLE OF CONTENTS

2009 River of Words ART FINALISTS

2009 River of Words TEACHER OF THE YEAR

Swan *by Atalanta Shi, age 13*
British Columbia, Canada
Submitted Independently

Unseen Secrets

I hide my secrets in the core of a brick
and on the surface of a star.

I tell my secrets to the unseen spirits around me
and the light rays from the sun.

Secrets live where man cannot go,
in the farthest part of space
and inside a velvet mite.

Quinn H. Whitlow, age 7
St. Louis Park, Minnesota
Homeschool
Teacher: Lisa Burger

2009 RIVER OF WORDS ART GRAND PRIZE WINNER
Category I (Grades K-2)

Killdeer by Jake Barrios, age 7
Watsonville, California   Watsonville Charter School of the Arts
Teachers: Alegra Bortin / Linda Cover

It's a Letter

In the dark blue sea
I saw a letter, it was

very small and this
is what it said:

I miss you in the dark blue sea.

I love to read but I need help
with some of the words.

I need help but I usually
read alone. I read one book

about Marvin becoming a king,
another book was about a shark.

Every time he sees legs or an arm
he goes into a wave and nothing

is there. Sometimes when I am
sad, I say *I hate my life.*

I run away, hide under the covers
And nothing is there but my book.

Yalonda Lockett, *age 9*
Lancaster, Pennsylvania
Fulton Elementary School
Teacher: Barbara Strasko

The Brown Bear in the Deep Cave by *Erik Raul Oliva, age 9*
Chico, California   Chico Country Day School
Teacher: Kari Zigan

Atmosphere

You gave your words
To the dog in the fall
Because he was new,
And you were still entertaining the idea
Of being an animal-lover.
And then in November,
When the lake was starting to get an icy sheen,
You sighed to your boyfriend
And let it echo through the rooms,
Even after he had left,
And you did not go down to the forest,
Whose bare trees were not welcoming,
But familiar,
Because you had sat in the piles of discarded leaves in autumn,
Just thinking.
Later it got cold,
And you weren't outside,
But cooped up by the TV
With all the lights in the house turned off,
And your face lit by the blue light of the screen,
While the weatherman once again announced that there would be snow.
And you do not remember the late fall grass,
Just turning brown,
Or the early winter trees,
Or when you were five,
And you paid attention to when you tread on brittle twigs,
Because you tried to avoid doing that
To honor the dead

Savannah Fehling, *age 14*
Sarasota, Florida
Booker Middle School
Teacher: Joanna Hapner-Fox

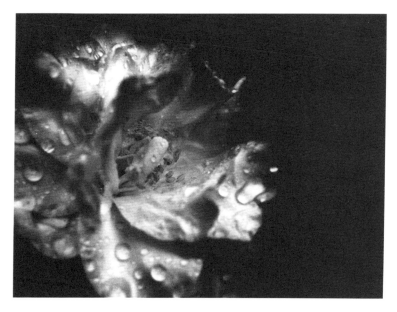

Night Flower *by Scott Styslinger, age 14*
Birmingham, Alabama   The Altamont School
Teacher: Marygray Hunter

2009 RIVER OF WORDS MONKEY'S RAINCOAT PRIZE
(Honoring a Short Poem in the Tradition of the Japanese Haiku)

Reflection

Yesterday,
I found a person just like me
in the frozen pond.

Noah Jordan, *age 9*
Alma, Maine
Center for Teaching & Learning (Edgecomb)
Teacher: Jill Cotta

Sisyphean

There was a time in my life
When I was the seagull, swallowing
Skin shed from all the flightless nights,
Sleepless nights. And everything
Seemed to resonate on the tips of my wings.

Then you came and laid a cold hand
On my head, fever nearly breaking my bones.
"Come on home," you whispered,
"the oaks are miserable without you."

And with that you returned to your home of leaves,
Made your bed with bees, and ate berries and seeds.
Meanwhile, I mended thirty pounds of weathered
Wings of all colors. I had been at the edge of the town,
Reattaching the chords and breaking the boards.
Carving wood had never been a hobby of mine,
But I carved ten trembling towers that day.

You rose to your feet, as I rose to the top of the heap.
Dusting off the dangling beads, you wrote
A piece about the stars, and the sky, and the clouds.
Then I cried, fell to blistered knees and wept
For each word and rhyme that tickled my ears.

Penitence is it, Sisyphus?
I'd gladly clamber up that horrid hill
With you, only you.

Skyler Pham, *age 17*
Opelousas, Louisiana
Magnet Academy for the Cultural Arts
Teacher: Holly Schullo

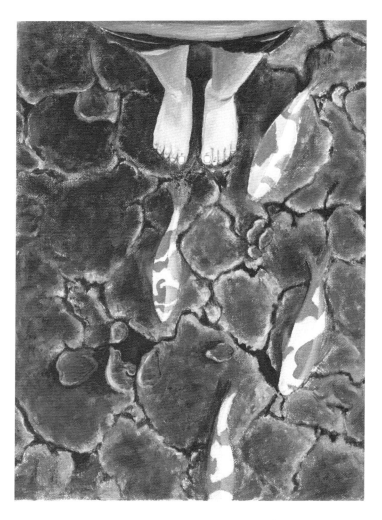

Remembered Water   *by Eunsil Choi, age 17*
Lawrenceville, Georgia   Parkview High School (Lilburn)
Teacher: Judy Nollner

Anacostia Shakespearean

Oh dear and lovely river of my dreams
I watch you sway and sing the world to sleep
I watch my childhood playing with the fish
I remember the crystals on the waves
The wildflowers that I picked in bouquets
You moan, but none can hear your quiet cry
You flowed to town from gentle hills above
You twist and turn, you slow to quench a thirst.
In winter I see tiny snowflakes fall
We fail to help you now and in the past
We fail, but we stand to try once again.
Some say that only god can make a tree
But rivers can be saved by kids like me.

Grace Fitzpatrick, *age 13*
Washington, DC
St. Peter's Interparish School
Teacher: Sandra Pierce

A Ship on a Dry Sea
by Jesse Abbott, age 15
Demorest, Georgia
Submitted Independently

18

Shadow Across The Moon

Moon,
        shining on the lake
gleaming under the headlights of the rusty Chevy
truck
        clamoring down the highway.
            The lake ripples.
The rock eroding down the mountain surrenders.
        Pines circle,
            water depends.
Another world.
        Another life.
            A wolf steps into the open
giving itself to the shadow across the moon.

Arianna LaChance, age 12
Mill Valley, California
Greenwood School
Teacher: Devika Brandt

Beauty in Numbers
by Addison Bandoly, age 8
Roswell, Georgia
Tritt Elementary
Teacher: Tamera Neal

19

What Water Says

The river to the West says "Raging"
The bog to the South says "Serene"
The sea to the East says "Rough"
The lake to the North says "Smooth"
The rain from the sky says "Light"
The ocean on the coast says "Heavy"
The spring from the ground says "Gushing"
The swamp in the wetland says "Still"
The puddle in the rainforest says "Shallow"
And the floor of the sea says "Profound"

Aidan Abney, *age 11*
Kokomo, Indiana
Sycamore Elementary School
Teacher: Scott Quinn

Frogs in the Pond *by Livia Korng, age 5*
Hong Kong, China   Renaissance College
Submitted Independently

Teaches

The sea brings me water
The moon helps me dream
The earth listens to my singing
The stars teach me how to dance

Bill Adams, *age 10*
Evans, Georgia
Columbia County 4-H (Martinez)
Facilitator: Shirley Williamson

Clean Water
by Morgen Dennis, age 9
Atlanta, Georgia
Oak Grove Elementary
Teacher: Beth Deery

The Johnny Pump Days

This was our childhood.
The sun pounding the scorched earth,
thirsty under our feet
as we fed it with our laughter
and the rain of the familiar hydrant that we called
our own.

This was our childhood
as our about-to-be-charred skin
beckoned us inside.
Stubborn, we basked in the glory of the
fleeting summer sun.

There we stood catching laughter as
resplendent drops of the
crystal-colored elixir
that we claimed as our own
bathed us with the secrets of that day.

Around and around we went
on that beloved street of our city,
ignorant of the delicious irony of a
red fire hydrant,
like water hidden in flame.

The milky magnolias and the
wisteria, kissed Tyrian hues,
graced us with their presence
on those days
as we ruled like kings and queens.
This was our childhood.

Obianujunwa Anakwenze, *age 17*
Florence, Alabama
Florence High School
Teacher: Darlene Freeman

Snowflake

Six-pointed wonder
Look at the blanket of snow
Snowmen start like this

Andrew Baxter, age 11
Gibsonia, Pennsylvania
Eden Hall Upper Elementary School
Teacher: Deborah Newcomer

My World

I stand on the moon
Looking at the big, round, blue earth
And I'm going to eat it
Very, very slowly.

Alexa Beaver, age 10
Fruita, Colordo
Caprock Academy (Grand Junction)
Teacher: Susan Sharpe

Water Paradise
by Lara Erjavec, age 13
Trbovlje, Slovenia
Teacher: Miroslava Kovacic

23

Ancient Language

The dragon's wings wave
across the brazen blue sky,
carving into the clouds
the story of the world
in the ancient tongue of fire.

On the ocean shore, the story
of the sea is written
along the cool brown sands
in the ancient language of water.

At High Noon the lurking shadow lingers
resting upon the green grassy glen.
A lazy comparison to the early morn,
when the swift shade swallows itself in swigs
in the ancient language of light.

Thornton Blease, *age 13*
Stewartsville, New Jersey
Homeschool
Teacher: Valerie Blease

The River of Beavers
by John Xuecheng Fan,
age 12
Ann Arbor, Michigan
The Art Corner
Teacher: Julee Li

A Precious Pearl

Amongst the folds of petals blue,
A sparkling jewel, a drop of dew.
It rests with sweet tranquility,
A precious pearl, for those who see.
Secrets of the garden pass,
Whispers in the dewy grass.
It forms before the sun awakes,
The morning mist a treasure makes.
The blue time, silent, peaceful rest,
It waits to shine to look its best.
It sparkles in the morning light,
So small and sweet, so kind and bright.
But with the smallest slight of hand,
It disappears into the land.
A moment's splendor lost in earth,
To rise and fall, a jewel's rebirth.

Mirabai Britton, *age 13*
Carmel, California
Carmel Middle School
Teacher: Liz Wells

Peace
Meranda Gaffney, age 15
Baltimore, Maryland
Good Shepherd School
Teacher: Ariadne Gejevski

Fourth Disappointment

She lies there, in her pink pajamas
on her mattress laid out on the
living room floor.
It's been there
ever since I've known her.
Crawling to the kitchen,
she still has a little bit of energy
to squat down and make kim-chee.
My great-grandmother,
named Fourth Disappointment,
who hardly talks or walks,
still smiles when I come
to see her.

Kyla Candido, *age 12*
Mill Valley, California
Greenwood School
Teacher: Devika Brandt

Raindrops by *Karmen Gaines, age 14*
Birmingham, Alabama   The Altamont School
Teacher: Marygray Hunter

• River of Words Poetry 2009 •

Lawn

gnomes,
plastic dinosaurs,
embellish the grass.
Randomly placed, standing in
a mess of garden furniture.
Bill and Ben the flowerpot men
wave hello to Snow White.
She is leaning to
one side, all
the way
across
the lawn
among her six
dwarfs, who lost a
brother in the tumult of
repainting the fence. What
a lovely way
to spend
a
Sunday afternoon.

Lizzie Chadbourne, age 12
Mill Valley, California
Greenwood School
Teacher: Devika Brandt

Mud
by Drake Harris, age 8
Marietta, Georgia
DueWest Elementary
Teachers: Lisa Slausen /
Stacey Harvey

27

To Lasso Grammar

They call these days
    The "dog days of summer"
Because dogs would lie down in the yard
    For a cat nap and never wake up.

I, too, may face the same, dark fate.
    I adjust the white Stetson on my head,
Hoping my sweat will glue the prized possession
    Safely over my carrot-colored top.

Not even the slimmest snake of a breeze
    Is here to wish me good luck.
I feel the evil heat laugh as the crowd in the arena
    Cheers ecstacially—my name's been called.

I quake in my duds as I'm handed my rope.
    "Thanks, Scotty," I whisper hoarsely
To my 12 year-young help.
    "Go get 'em," he tells me with his eyes alight.

The look from those blazing blue spheres
    And the feel of the familiar, coarse rope
In my weathered, cowboy hands
    Are all it takes for my instinct to snap back into place.

With my chin held high as the rusted door is noisily lifted up
    I squint menacingly at the fan-filled arena
And spot my goal scraping its hooves in the dirt across the ring.
    There lies the wild, unbridled mustang named Poetry.

Jenae' Clay, age 17
Lafayette, Louisiana
Lafayette High School
Teacher: Laurie Godshall

Turtles

Overlooked
Underestimated
Filled to the brim with low expectations

Split-vision migraines
from reconciling Kingdom, Phylum, Sub-Phylum, Class,
Order, Family, Genus, Species
with the poetry of each maze-patterned shell

I see the organism and the metaphor
The science and the ideal
I just can't see the simple, contented box turtle
half hidden in the grass

Overlooked
Underestimated
But their shallow depths go over my head

Caroline Devlin, *age 16*
Baton Rouge, Louisiana
Louisiana State University Lab School
Teacher: Connie MacDonald

My Home, My Country
by Vanessa Ho, age 13
Hong Kong, China
Diocesan Girls' School
Teacher: Pearl Kam

Afternoon

I smelled lavender
In an evergreen forest

I felt the ocean tide
Curling around my ankles
Bringing golden sand
To play around my feet

I saw a flamingo
Dip its head low to the water
And waltz with its reflection

I heard D Minor
Pirouette up my finger
And rest gently on my heart

Helena Eitel, *age13*
Seattle, Washington
Lakeside Middle School
Teacher: Alicia Hokanson

Rainbow Rock Fish
by Patrick Kam, age 9
Silver Spring, Maryland
Forest Knolls Elementary
Teacher: Maria Ferrari

Smokey Mountains

These mountains are always changing.
They brace against winter,
To sprout leaves of green
And shed them red and gold.
They stand as brothers to fight the wind
That rolls through this valley of smoke.

There's a river that runs through these mountains,
Carving its way through granite and stone.
She runs, not in a hurry, but slows to enjoy the ride
Forever she flows through the ages and times,
For the entire world, a pretty view.

Birds that are singing,
Deer that go running,
And turkeys that act like they're kings
They all find a home here,
Just like me.

Amelia Fuller, *age 12*
Jefferson, North Carolina
Homeschool
Teacher: Marjorie Fuller

Hard Worker
by Sakina Khadimi, age 16
Quetta, Pakistan
(Afghan national)
Ghulghula Art Gallery
Teacher: Hassan Ali Hatif

31

The Dog

```
S
W
I
S
H                              R
S                            A   F
 W                          F     S
  I                        R   O      See Sniffle
   S                          A   F              S
    Huff Huff Huff Huff Huff   R   Jaw        LL E M
    Huff Huff Huff Huff Huff  A
    Huff Huff   Huff Huff
       Huff      Huff
        R         R
        U         U
        N         N
       RUN       RUN
```

Paul Harrington, Age 10
Holland, Michigan
Lakewood Elementary School
Teacher: Debbie Whitbeck

Coyote
Daniel Knight, age 7
Watsonville, California
Watsonville Charter
School of the Arts
Teachers: Manjula
Stokes / Linda Cover

Island Life

Island cars sputter and jolt
along narrow winding island lanes.
Plumes of smoke come out
of the tailpipe with each bump.
Dents pock mark the metal sides of the paint job
that has slowly changed from forest green,
to navy blue, to fire hydrant red to a dried blood rust,
like weeds overpowering a garden.
Bumpers drag along the road
behind cars.

Roads with different colors and textures of tar
overlap each other like a quilt,
you're lucky if they're even paved.
Scattered along the road are the well known potholes
gaping like craters.

Boxes of toilet paper, coke, and beer heave off the ferry.
Plastic bag handles strain, taut with tension.
People struggle with Hannaford and Shaw's bags.
Frail looking old ladies pull immense amounts of food,
their biceps strengthened from this weekly work out.
They never seem disheartened by this chore;
they never grumble or whine.

Old islanders go to the General Store to gossip
simply because they have nothing better to do.
Kids roam like nomads on bikes,
traveling in packs, clouds of dust forming behind them.
People amble leisurely down the road,
stopping here and there to talk.

Because why hurry?

Tess Hinchman, *age 12*
West Bath, Maine
Center for Teaching & Learning (Edgecomb)
Teacher: Glenn Powers

reflection

perhaps when i am close to being gone
and returning to this earth
i will say i want to be like livingstone
take my body where you will but
bury my heart beneath
this obsidian soil
against a layer of warm limestone
where the river is the clearest
of mirrors

Jennifer Hu, *age 16*
Hummelstown, Pennsylvania
Hershey High School

Untitled *by Marqusha Oliver, age 12*
Kansas City, Missouri   Lee A. Tolbert Community Academy
Teacher: J. Yocum

34

Five Favorite Things
(From a Five-Year-Old)

Things that are red,
Sleeping in my parents' bed,
Books that I have read,
My dog when she is fed,
Thinking thoughts in my head.

Everett Hutter, *age 5*
Bethesda, Maryland
Homeschool
Teacher: Michelle Hutter

Here or There

In a diverse world,
A world of narrow alleys,
And of wide open green space,
One where the old,
Must accommodate the new,
Where speeders,
Must tolerate the loafers,
We return to our roots,
To learn the strength of our branches.

David Lauve, *age 18*
Baton Rouge, Louisiana
Louisiana State University Lab School
Teacher: Candence Robillard

Clean Water
by Alexandra Laing, age 9
Atlanta, Georgia
Oak Grove Elementary School
Teacher: Beth Deery

35

Ode to the Tangerine

Slowly
peeling the outer shell
to discover
a world
of veins and
crystals frozen
in juice

Complicated
unexplained designs
woven of cells
mitochondria
golgi apparatus.

A world
orbiting
its own sun
still undiscovered by
scientists
full of instruments to
measure eternity
but lacking
a sense of taste.

And in the middle of the conjunction
of cells
suns and castles
in a single seed
are found
the mysteries
of infinite
space.

Oda a la Mandarina

Lentamente
abriendo la cáscara
para descubrir
un mundo
de venas y
cristales congeladas
en jugo.

Complicados
diseños inexplicados
tejido de células
mitocondria
aparatos golgi.

Un mundo
orbitando
su propia sol
que todavía no se han descubierto
científicos
llenos de instrumentos para
medir eteridad
pero faltando
un sentido de sabor.

Y en medio del conjunto
de células,
soles y castillos,
en una semilla
se encuentra
los misterios
del
espacio
infinito.

Audrey Larkin, age 15
San Francisco, California
Poetry Inside Out
Teacher: John Oliver Simon

• River of Words Poetry 2009 •

The Heart of the Hibiscus

is a promise
of sunlight

or a forgiving
shade of pink

or maybe a window
at the moment

of sweet moring,
clear horizon,

pure warmth,
bright sky.

Cyrus Maunakea, *age 11*
Honolulu, Hawaii
Na'au School
Teacher: Lois-Ann Yamanaka

Picture (Almost) Perfect *by Tiffany Ling, age 16*
Lilburn, Georgia   Parkview High School
Teacher: Judy Nollner

Genesis

It's been a long time since I came here
last, and I can't seem to remember why I
had stayed away for so long; none of my
excuses—time, school, more time—seem to
live up to their purpose. What seems like

so long ago I came here with my sister,
each of us too old to hold hands, and too
jaded to even try, and we walked along the
bridges and the sidewalks, stopping to watch
the magnificently brown water bubble past

as it traipsed like fine ladies by the park.
I never could understand, even then, how
such a trivial thing could become so perfect,
but, as I watch the reeds sway under the slight
waves, and the spines of fish slice by the
under-bellies of blue canoes, I realize that

it was never a matter of importance. This river
has always been a place for all those things
transitory. My life, my feelings, my friends.
Only that one thing, the most important, has
ever withstood the mark of this river. My family.
I can see here, on the west bank, my nephew's
sixth birthday, and there, by the fishing dock,
a picnic in July. Far away, dozing on the rocky

shore, small salamanders whose skin seems to
bronze even darker in the setting sun. There is
no way to fully explain how these waters have
truly, uniquely shaped my life, but I can, finally
just see how I was carved around it, in rivulets
and how, though I was not borne from it,

I have become it.

Megan Mabry, *age 16*
Roswell, Georgia
Roswell High School
Teacher: Joel McElvaney

The Days of Glory

Something to write about.
Something to sing about.
Something to think about
in the clouds above us
in the night sky.

Over stars and past the moon,
past the days of glory.

Madeline McGrigg, age 7
Denver, Colorado
Polaris @ Ebert
Teacher: Karin Johnson

Notan Beach by Hannah McGee, age 17
Huntsville, Alabama   Madison Academy (Madison)
Teacher: Peggy Hickerson

Koi Pond: Persona of My Music Teacher

Like oil, suspended in droplets
The size of copper coins
Plunked by well-wishers,
The sunlight waits to be
Swept up in your childhood pail,
Dipped beneath the surface to scatter
The swarming calico scales,
Trembling the pond with their
Frantic wriggling delight.
But it is a calm,
Contained by the fern fronds
And mossy stones,
Warm as golden tabbies, whose tails
Have curled under their noses.
A breath, testing its persistence,
Ripples through the pond
Like a shudder
As a koi breaks the surface,
Fluorescent scales trailing behind
In fragments and chips of color,
Dispersed in the evening's murky water.

Emilie Menzel, *age 16*
Lilburn, Georgia
Parkview High School
Teacher: Mary Lynn Huie

Kennebec Pantoum

Steam rolls off the river
Snow slides down its banks
and stifles
brown grass.

Snow slides down its banks.
Old leaves dance on
brown grass,
leaving the maples lonely.

Old leaves dance on
frosted rooftops,
leaving maples lonely
with the weight of winter.

Frosted rooftops
sag and leak
with the weight of winter
along my stony Kennebec.

Emma Moorhead, *age 13*
Bath, Maine
Center for Teaching & Learning (Edgecomb)
Teacher: Nancie Atwell

Colourfull River
by Sasini Navoda
Wickramatunga,
age 10
Colombo, Sri Lanka
Sampath Rekha
International
Art Academy
Teacher:
Hasanthi Sarada
Bogahawatta

41

Rattlesnake

Rattlesnakes are packed with lots of colors,
no legs, and bad habits
They have tails to shake at you
so you won't die

Cole Morales, age 7
Laguna Niguel, California
Malcolm Elementary School
Teacher: Elisa Slee

Untitled

Lost in the gutter
Disowned shadows flit across
Remnants of childhood

Bo Yan J. Moran, age 14
San Francisco, California
Lick-Wilmerding High School
Teacher: Tamara Pellicier

The Pond Behind My House

The pond behind my house
sits quietly rippling, shallow and dark.
Like her siblings the rivers, oceans and lakes,
a lover of rain and fresh melting snow.
She fears the sun—a slow hot demise,
and thirsts for water—a random revival.
A sliver of calm tucked into new urban sprawl,
fish, turtles and frogs—they make her their home.
She resides in a woodlot just bigger than she is,
the pond behind my house.

Ruben Moreno, age 10
Silver Spring, Maryland
St. Andrew Apostle School

42

Harvested

No one to hear us,
we pack the cavernous night
with our voices—
the breeze that ruffles the reeds
carries our conversation
across the moon-paled marsh.
Odd spurts of song and laughter echo
up the paved hill where tree shadows
connect with ours
to create kaleidoscopic designs
on the asphalt.

On the journey home
we slip into comfortable silence
wade through the pool of rusty lamp light,
and emerge under a star-studded sky.
We tilt our faces
to greet the winking points,
and you and I breathe deep to harvest
this moment with each other
and the patterns etched above.

Amelia Neilson, age 14
Arrowsic, Maine
Center for Teaching & Learning
(Edgecomb)
Teacher: Nancie Atwell

Seashore at Full
Moonlight
by Prakruthi, age 10
Bangalore, India
Lalithkala Academy
of Fine Arts Education
Teacher: Vinu Kumar

43

Bullhead

Dark
bullhead shark
attacks
unlucky
crab and shellfish
along the shores
of Haleiwa Beach.
Its head
is SOOOOOO
BIG
but not as big
as a hammerhead.
Powerful
tail, thrashing
it toward
a shellfish.
Its big head
helps it
find food
and sharp
razor teeth
kill its prey.

Sidney Pang, *age 10*
Honolulu, Hawaii
Na 'au School
Teacher: Lois-Ann Yamanaka

**Bird Playing with
an Elephant**
*by H. N. Rathnayaka,
age 11
Columbo, Sri Lanka
Sampath Rekha
International
Art Academy
Teacher: Hasanthi
Sarada Bogahawatta*

The Island

They mowed the meadows down below
Our house the other day,
But left a grassy island where
We still can go and play.

Right in the middle of the field
It rises green and high;
Bees swing on the clover there,
And butterflies blow by.

It seems a very far-off place
With oceans all around;
The only thing to see is sky,
And wind the only sound.

Georgina Parfitt, *age 10*
San Ramon, California
Dorris-Eaton School (Walnut Creek)
Teacher: Jennifer Lynn

Deer
by Jacob Scott, age 12
Tell City, Indiana
Tell City Junior High
Teacher: Kyle Miles

Behind Our School

Behind our school
We made a loft in a tree with six trunks
Found an old railroad nail
And a fire poker
Spent a long time finding branches
And cutting them in half
We called it our chimpanzee nest.

Behind our school
You can make forts
Cross a marsh
Run from hornets
Build a swing
See the source of the little stream
Lay in a meadow
Explore in the pine needle forest
Look over a cliff
Spot foxes
Watch out for a bear
Follow deer tracks
Find an old house
Find a creepy old campsite
Run away from dogs
Come across a waterfall
Slip in the mud
Climb on fallen trees
Take a stream walk and end up swimming in it
Find an arrowhead
Feel relaxed
Calm
Tranquil
Happy
Grateful

Samah Rash, *age 11*
Bedford, Virginia
World Community Education Center
Teacher: Linda Ingram

Child Kingdom *by Muzhgan, age 13*
Quetta, Pakistan (Afghan national)   Ghulghula Art Gallery
Teacher: Hassan Ali Hatif

Of Purple

Today I washed my dog with purple shampoo,
some fancy stuff that probably wasn't meant for dogs.
When I rinsed him, the whole tub turned
swirling, dusky purple
like you might see in a sunset after a grey day.
Or like a dress I once tried on:
it reminded me of Shakespeare and dancing and poetry,
but when I put it on, it looked awful,
kind of like my wet dog and the hairy tub and the dripping bottle
once I was finished.
All that was left were vaguely purple soap suds
and a little less water in Lake Lanier.
The shampoo bottle still lay on the counter
atop a little pool of dark, shiny velvet that had melted into goo
which could, I knew, transform
back into the violet shadows where fairies tread,
or so they say.
I left it, and dried off my dog.
But it was pretty, that purple.

Hope Rogers, *age 17*
Lilburn, Georgia
Parkview High School
Teacher: Mary Lynn Huie

Clear

Smooth green water
swirls past my fingertips
I cut through the clear,
glassy surface,
and feel the river tempt the heat
of August
down to the icy,
pebbled bottom.

Aurora Rummel-Lindig, age 13
Missoula, Montana
Sussex School
Teacher: Jennifer Ellis

Rural India Morning,
Indian Tea
by Shruthi S., age 14
Bangalore, India
Mary Immaculate School
Teacher: Mudassir N. Shaik

49

The air

is something

growing

inside of me,

like a story

about a flower.

Alijah Rosario, *age 8*
Lancaster, Pennsylvania
Fulton Elementary School
Teacher: Barbara Strasko

Resting
by N.S.K. Silva, age 12
Colombo, Sri Lanka
Sampath Rekha
International
Art Academy
Teacher: Hasanthi
Sarada Bogahawatta

Ars Poetica

Poetry cannot be created;
it must be found—
discovered in the smile emanating from the old man's eyes
when he pours the water at the local Thai restaurant,
in my friends' laughter after football games—
climbing the fence and navigating the trail
to reach Hope's house,
then talking in the driveway until midnight curfew
sends us all scurrying home.

Poetry lingers, waiting to be noticed
in the clear sky before I leave for school,
in the feel of my dog's tongue when she licks my fingers,
in the ninety-nine cent vanilla milk at the gas station.

But sometimes poetry hides,
wishing it were not in
the inevitable college rejection letter
or the CNN special on genocides—
the one that left me crying on my bed
long after my parents thought I was asleep—
or in the old man's absence
the last few times my family went out to eat.

Courtney Reed, *age 18*
Lilburn, Georgia
Parkview High School
Teacher: Mary Lynn Huie

You Got Lost Inside an Afternoon

Ashes bled into your fingers
as you searched
for Petoskey. Your dog
trotted ahead of you,
tail waving under the grainy sky.
Soon it began to rain.
The lake embraced puddles
that formed on the shore
where you walked, your shoes
muddy, your heart
content. Sometimes
in your dreams

you find yourself standing
on that wet beach
with shells in your hand,
the dunes pressed up so tightly
against the sky, trees dripping
rainwater. Sometimes you dream
that an egret calls in the distance,
once,
twice,
then silence.

Patricia Schlutt, *age 14*
Grand Rapids, Michigan
Rodney Torreson's Poetry Workshop
Teacher: Rodney Torreson

Bluebird and its Berry
by Grace Tran, age 7
Creative Minds Art Studio
Portland, Oregon
Teacher: Wanda Ng

In the Mountains

One night the rain fell so hard
that we thought the sky had been torn open
and was bleeding its last lifeblood over our crops,
crippling the shack where we lived:
half the roof fell in and we huddled
in the cellar among rotting carrots,
mud running down the cold stone
from the cracks in the cellar door.
It was past midnight and the rain still bit
chunks out of the hillside,
the dark sky empty
thickened with water, empty of stars
so we slept in the cellar, uneasy,
and when the rain finally stopped
hours later, it was still dark
and we woke to the mourning of wolves
somewhere deeper out in the forest.

Patricia Schlutt, *age 14*
Grand Rapids, Michigan

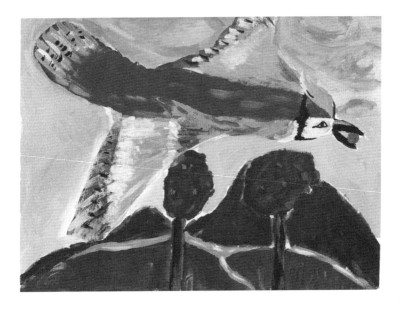

Leap of Faith

Dripping sun
gripping the ripple
of infinite
ploosh.

Biting sky,
beckoning the need
to leave
to be found.

Cascading patches
of feathered hope,
flapping away
sameness.

Wind beaten wings,
ripping the edge
of unstable fantasy.

Leaping

Flying

Flying

Soaring

Elisa Steele, *age 12*
Kirkwood, Missouri
North Kirkwood Middle School
Teacher: Melissa Banjak

Chinese Opera Artist
by Wong Cho Ying, age 8
Hong Kong, China
Simply Art
Teachers: Lau Hoo Cheong / Lee Chui San

Evening, Night

The sun
falls behind
the hills
as the sky
turns black
and the stars start
to explore the darkness.

Ariah Thornton, *age 10*
Sonoma, California
Prestwood Elementary School
Teacher: Anne Estes

Swimming in the Sea by *Zachary Tomlinson, age 8*
Siler City, North Carolina   Homeschool

Just Because

Just because there is a brook,
doesn't mean there is a river. Just
because there is a river, doesn't mean
there is a lake. Just because there
is a lake doesn't mean there is an
ocean. Just because there is an ocean
doesn't mean you can't dream.

Jullisa Trevino, age 12
Tucson, Arizona
Challenger School
Teacher: Mrs. Olson

Wading to the Water *by Joshua Vega, age 18*
Hollister, California   San Benito High School
Teacher: John Robrock

You, Lake

You, lake, pale and kissed by twilight,
Let me sit for just an hour more
Until the stars whisper their fast approach.

I am like you, who gathers the rain and quietly
sends it back,
Who lets the fall leaves rot on the shore,
Who is always touched by wind.

We drift through the seasons together without
thought or grievance,
And I always wonder how deep you go.
Someday, I know, I will find you lowest valley,

And in all that green water, in all the tangled
weeds and oil,
The lost oars and drowned roots,
I will find your deep connection to the world.

Matt Turner, age 17
Kenmore, Washington
Inglemoor High School
Teacher: Tim Curtis

Don't Be Coy
by Juan Velasquez,
age 17
Hollister,
California
San Benito
High School
Teacher: John
Robrock

To a Cabin-I

Only space
for those in need of sea
and sky;
Only room for those in need of infinity.
Fennel
Lupine
Sage
ripen on tumbles of rocks.
Cormorant
King Fisher
Gull
Glide on waves of foam.
Splashing against
a life distilled;
a spare sanctuary—
To a cabin, we must go.

To a Cabin-II

A narrow road:
the gate, the ridge, the bridge
only space,
only room, for those in need of clarity.
Run through
Brush
Bracken
Poppies.

Comb
Cut
Kill
out complexities,
Setting
and
Soothing,
Reminding
and
Replacing
with lessons in simplicity—
Survival.

To a Cabin-III

Every day,
Every night,
chasing sidewalks,
another moon covered in fog
waits,
without fail,
for our return.
Our desire names them:
Whale rock,
Wildflower ridge,
Lower meadow,
Crescent stone,
Vista Boulder—
our meeting place
with windows facing the sea,
where waves have different voices
lurching
against incomparable rocks—
altered,
off-beat—
a variety of sounds—
of rumble,
wheeze,
and whir—
To a cabin, we must go.

To a Cabin-IV

Tonight,
climbing Sea-Scarred boulders
isn't enough
Nor is toe-tag or foot-fighting
with the surf—
sand against salty flesh,
along the scalloped border.
Tonight—
my hands are on fire from
fringed surf, crisp
on knees, thighs and torso.
Tonight,
must be enough to run back to
the grain of stone and pebbles,
pressed
into the Sea-Scarred boulder,
only to find you
sinking with me into the silent,
still-warm-from-daylight stone,
your hand gliding along
glistening, numb skin,
resting
and rising
against my chest.

Marley Walker, age 15
San Francisco, California

A River
by Prasadini Wickramasinghe,
age 13
Mawanella, Sri Lanka
Mahamya Girls' College

Majesty by Lucy Xu, age 17
Lilburn, Georgia   Shijun Art Studio
Teacher: Shijun Munns

2009
River of Words
Teacher of the Year
Barbara Strasko

Fulton Elementary School
Lancaster, Pennsylvania

Barbara Buckman Strasko is a Literacy Coach at the Fulton Elementary School, in the School District of Lancaster in Pennsylvania. In 2008, she was appointed Poet Laureate of Lancaster County by the Lancaster Literary Guild. Her poems have appeared in *The Best New Poets of 2006*, *Rhino*, *Spoon River Poetry Review*, *Tar River Poetry Review*, *Ellipsis* and *Ninth Letter*. Her chapbook *On the Edge of a Delicate Day* was published by Pudding House Press.

Barbara Strasko earned her MFA in Creative Writing from the Vermont College of Fine Arts. Strasko is also a graduate of Millersville University where she earned a BS in Elementary Education / Special Education, a Reading Specialist certification, Early Childhood Education and Guidance Certification, as well as an MS in Psychology. She was a guidance counselor for many years.

Barbara Strasko grew up in Bucks County, Pennsylvania, an area rich in the arts. In college she was a volunteer tutor in a largely Spanish-speaking educational center and began a career teaching in the School District of Lancaster. For many years she lived in the city and now she lives at the edge of the Conestoga River. She continues to pursue her love for nature, teaching, counseling and working in the community.

Barbara Strasko teaches poetry as a catalyst for literacy and achievement in academics and the arts, in a high-poverty urban school. She coordinates a student performance called Poetry and Arts Night for her school and community each year and she also edits *Sunrise*, the Fulton School Art & Literary magazine.

As a poet-educator, Barbara Strasko uses the language of poetry to promote sensitivity, self-expression and healing. She believes poetry teaches us to observe closely, to appreciate beauty and to further understand human emotions. In her artistic statement she says, "I see a poem as a moment of change, and think the writing of poetry is a powerful way to shift our perceptions of ourselves and the world."

Through the River of Words curriculum and contest Strasko feels she is better able to motivate her students to write poems, and that it gives them a way to show the world what they know and what they want to change.

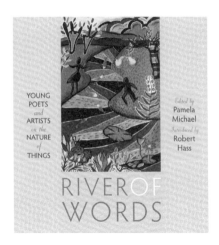

*If you're in the Bay Area, please visit
River of Words' new gallery—
one of the first in the country
devoted exclusively to
the work of young people.*

Young at Art
GALLERY

**CHILDREN'S ART & POETRY
FROM AROUND THE WORLD**

*Prints, original art, notecards and more
Unique, affordable and amazing!*

*To view all this year's winning artwork, please visit
www.riverofwords.org,
or visit
River of Words' Young At Art Gallery
933 Parker Street, Studio 38
Berkeley, California*

(Call for hours or to make appointment 510-548-7636)

YETI: THE ABOMINABLE SNOWFLAKE

January 1998—August 2008

Yeti went to work at River of Words with me almost every weekday of her too short life. A Tibetan Terrier bred to keep the feet of meditating monks warm under their robes in the Himalayan cold, she carried out her genetic imperative by insisting on sleeping on my feet in the footwell of my desk, constantly risking injury by the "wheels of death"—an office chair piloted by a rather large woman who was often in motion.

It's difficult to describe the bonds at work in a "pack of two," as Yeti and I were. She saw details of nature and daily living I would have missed, were it not for her keen attention.

She taught me much about unconditional love and devotion, and kept me mindful of the complicated and beautiful connection between humans and wildness.

In her role as "office dog," she entertained countless visitors to the River of Words office over the years, and attended many workshops, festivals, and board meetings, often sitting in a chair at the board table, attentive to whomever was speaking. As a tiny puppy, she even attended a Public Utilities Commission meeting, secretly tucked into my blouse, somehow aware she had to be silent.

She was a funny, wise, head-strong little spirit who made my days, and especially my walks, vibrant and alive. She is missed.

Pamela Michael

photo by Glen Billy